P9-DUX-384

Grandpa Was No Saint

---

poems

James P. Quinn

FITHIAN PRESS ♦ SANTA BARBARA ♦ 1995

Many of the poems in this book have appeared previously in the same or slightly altered form in the following periodicals:

Archer, Bad Haircut Quarterly, Bean Feast, Broken Streets, Connecticut River Review, Deros, Dusty Dog, Echoes, Exit 13, Feelings, Grasslands Review, Heartland Journal, Hobo Jungle, Innisfree, Jefferson Review, Manna, Odessa Poetry Review, Old Hickory Review, Orphic Lute, Parnassus, Poetic Justice, Poetry Magic, Prophetic Voices, Psychopoetica, Skylark, Sovereign Gold, Tara's Arts Journal, Thirteen, Z Miscellaneous.

Copyright © 1995 by James P. Quinn
All rights reserved
Printed in the United States of America

Published by Fithian Press
A division of Daniel and Daniel, Publishers, Inc.
Post Office Box 1525
Santa Barbara, CA 93102

Book design by Eric Larson

LIBRARY OF CONGRESS CATALOGING-IN-PUBLICATION DATA
Quinn, James P.
    Grandpa was no saint / James P. Quinn
      p.   cm.
    ISBN 1-56474-136-2
    1. Irish American families—Poetry.
    2. Family—United States—Poetry.
    3. Irish Americans—Poetry I. Title
PS3567.U344G73   1995
811'.54—dc20   94-48845
                                            CIP

Dedicated to my wife, Pat—
the guardian of our dreams
and the keeper of the flame.

CONTENTS

I. Family Secrets

There is a land of the living and a land of the dead and the bridge is love, the only survival, the only meaning.

—THORNTON WILDER

KITCHEN MUSIC

for Genevieve

Today mother would have sung
the blues to hear her kitchen so quiet.
So many sounds have filled this room:
I still recall the tea kettle singing
us awake every morning and songs
of children playing filtering
through the window and suppertime
voices flying around the kitchen table
trading tales about family and friends
burdened with more than their share
of happiness or grief. All the while
we're talking the clinking of plates
and dishes as mother serves up
the corned beef and cabbage.
After supper, sister, up to her elbows
in soap suds, humming a melody
in contrast to father's silent tune.
But always mother's laughter—music
to our bruised egos and skinned shins.
And this song for you my family.

MOTHER'S HANDS

for Florence

Were like wild birds
delicate and ubiquitous.
How often
and in what detail
I dream about them
working a steam iron
over a pair of trousers
scrubbing mirror circles
on the kitchen floor
sending out wash
on the noisy clothesline
rolling pie crusts
thin as a wafer
pouring tea with the solemnity
of a priest distributing communion
fingering each bead
like an apple-cheeked novitiate
waving farewells
from the porch window
clutching that still crucifix
with jewels of ice.

A RAILROADER'S MORNING

for Vince

Sometimes when the alarm goes off
on a winter morning, I linger under the blanket
and remember how the old man never needed
an alarm clock. He'd rise with the whistle

of the early freight bound for Buffalo.
In his loud Irish voice, typical of men who work
too many years in the deafening noise of the freight yard,
he'd say, *Flo, don't keep supper. I'll be working overtime.*

I'd hear him stumble around the room trying
to get his crippled legs into the patched coveralls.
Then he'd wind the gold pocket watch, given to him
by his father, counting aloud each turn.

All the while I'd lie awake in the dark listening
for his heavy shoes creaking down the stairs,
the tea kettle's shrill whistle, the backdoor slamming.
When the old Plymouth's engine finally cranked over

I'd drift back to sleep and dream of the whistle-ports
this land-sailor would make before his return.

WE DIDN'T OWN A T.V.

for Vince

That's why my old man would take me
to the Front Street Tavern
to watch the week's major event:
the Friday night fights.
I'd sit in the corner
my small hand wrapped around
a frosted mug of sarsaparilla
dreaming about the great ones,
explosive, ablaze with their fists
defending championship belts and manhood
for our pleasure: Louis-Walcott, LaMotta-Robinson,
Pep-Saddler, feeling at home
with the Pabst Blue Ribbon sign
blinking in the front window
and the smell of stale beer mixed
with the scent of sawdust and cigar smoke.
I'd listen to Fats Domino belt out
Blueberry Hill on the jukebox amid the shouts
of shuffleboard players demanding refills
pushing their basketball bellies, large, round,
cultivated by a lifetime of beer guzzling,
against the polished mahogany bar
shining so you could see your reflection.

I'd watch the tattooed young men,
greased hair combed into ducktails
cigarettes rolled in T-shirt sleeves,
playing pool in the back room
talking loud and tough
trying to impress the young women
sitting at tables drinking rum and cokes
wearing their tight sweaters
and too much lipstick
the color of crushed cherries.
God, I just loved this world
of sounds smells moving bodies
drawn together once a week
to worship the talking box
tucked under the ceiling
at the end of the bar.

GRANDPA WAS NO SAINT

for Tom Smith

Most mornings I'd find him
bent over the kitchen table
a long ash of a Camel dangling,
an ear cocked to the radio,
the paper open to the racing charts.

But his afternoons were a ritual:
after checking his shoes, tie
and fedora, he'd struggle
down three flights and walk four
blocks to the Front Street Tavern.

Here, sitting with the regulars,
he'd sip Scotch whiskey neat
without ever spilling a drop.
After several hands of poker,
he'd begin the Glasgow stories.

The blinking neon sign told him
it was time for his nightcap.
He'd drink it off cleanly, slip
the barman a few bucks
and walk out with dignity intact.

A FASTIDIOUSNESS FOR ORDER

for Claire

Was her attempt to turn
an upside down world
into a structured illusion.

Each day was planned
like a perfectly
synchronized marching band
never out of step.

Hours bent over
the kitchen sink
arms sunk in soap suds.

Cabinets meticulously arrayed
like regiments
waiting for inspection.

The insatiable feeding
of almost-clean clothes
load after load
into the old Kenmore.

An eternity spent
at the ironing board each
shirt sleeve affectionately
pressed and folded.

Only the endless pieces
of shattered dreams littered
her glossy linoleum floor.

THE PRODIGAL SON

Mother's bedroom was mostly a shrine
and every day she'd call herself to vespers.
Pictures of the Sacred Heart stared
down from all four walls.

On the dresser holy water
and a small crystal vase
filled with plastic flowers
paid homage to the Virgin's statue.

Her worn rosary beads hanging
from the bedpost gave evidence
of a morning ritual like the yellow-thumbed
pages of *Lives of the Saints*.

Almost daily she'd record an inspirational
entry into her leather-bound diary
like how the prodigal son is weak, must
always be taken in and protected.

I remember one dark winter night
the prodigal son came home drunk
cursing his brother. Mother said
I ought to leave to avoid a conflict.

That night I wanted so much
to be the prodigal son.
At least, he wasn't the one
being sent out into the cold.

HOMECOMING

Why you've returned
to the old neighborhood
you'll never know
since there's nothing
to show you once lived here.
You don't remember
the street being so narrow
or the houses so small.
Strange faces bustle past
and not one old neighbor is left.
In Swartz's grocery window
the neon sign is written
in an unfamiliar language.
Even the old clapboard homestead
is hardly recognizable
in its shiny new suit of siding.
Maybe the ducks at Cooper's Pond
or the ghosts in the Old South cemetery
will remember you?

SON TO FATHER

for Vince

In my tortured half-sleep
you come back to me
across the shadow-light of dream.
As your disembodied form crystallizes
into human time and space
we stand like mirror images
on each side of the bridge
facing one another in silence.
Now you don't seem ashamed
to walk over, grab me by the shoulders,
pull me to your breast.
I always knew that granite handshake
was your way of saying *I love you.*

II. Beginnings

*Poetry is my way of exploring my
own spiritual journey, and,
I hope, the spiritual journey of the
reader.*

—ERICA JONG

PROMISE RENEWED

for Mike

The glare from Achilles' shield
breaks through the budding trees
painting the hillside with beginnings.
Amid a sea of fresh green
wild young dandelions
bend yellow in the wind.
Overhead longnecks wing-flapping
home with excited blood
honk a friendly welcome.
Air strewn with the smell
of honeysuckle purifies
like altar incense.

Heaven has kept its promise.

THE GARDEN

for Cheryl and Jim, October 3, 1987

A marriage like a garden
must be cultivated and nurtured.
When the heart is furrowed
and the sacred vows planted deep
as seedlings in fertile ground
a love rooted in the flesh
will blossom into a mystical
union of souls. In time
the travails of the world
will try to destroy this flower
like a killer blight separates
the petals from the stem.
But faith in His light
will regenerate the marriage
as water running under ground
gives life to the roots
and love will continue to raise
its unique delicate presence
like the mysterious flower
that pushes upward through stone
unfolding its petals of joy.

PLAYGROUND

It's their shrill voices
that draw his attention
little gossipers squealing
in the vernacular of joy
the passionate beginning of things.
He observes them at play working
tricycles over hallowed ground
in ever expanding circles
climbing the slide ladder
a little closer to heaven
swinging back and forth
higher and higher drifting
above time and meaning.
Let them be happy. Soon enough
life's deeply buried knowledge
will flash clear before them
turning innocent eyes to tears
closing up the circles
tumbling them into time
sending them screaming to earth.

INNOCENCE

When the weary routine
of school came to an end
he'd stash his books under the forsythia
inside the cemetery fence
and cut across to Cooper's Pond.
On these warm spring afternoons
fishing at the old mill attracted him
like a trout jumps at a lure.
Wearing the sun on his back
bare feet dangling over the dam's edge
waterfall swishing between his toes
he'd spend hours staring down
at golden carp moving lazily to and fro
under the water's glassy surface.
It must have been the sound
of voices that drew his attention
to the adjacent marsh.
Pushing aside the willow branches
he silently observed them
his young mind trying
to comprehend the scene.
When their eyes met his
they were transfixed
like Aphrodite and Ares
caught in Hephaistos' net.
"Hey kid," was all he heard
as he ran bewildered
through a maze of cattails.
It was many years before
he understood why Miss Driscol
called him a *dirty boy* and tore
his drawing into tiny pieces.

BEYOND BLUE

for Jimmy

There was never a moment
quite like the one we shared
holding you for the first time.

All strawberries and cream
as I cradled you so close and felt
the rhythm of your heartbeat.

I watched your patient mouth
tug gently at the bottle
not hurrying your feast

and the way that smile
danced across your face
gathering in the sweetness.

Looking into those bright blue eyes
I knew the mountains didn't melt
or the birds forget to fly

I just caught my first glimpse of heaven.

DOC'S

for Bob & Rose

Just a short distance
from the railroad crossing
on West Main Street
there's a bicycle shop where
a pharmacy used to be located.
Doc's was an old-fashioned drugstore
complete with wooden barrels filled
with hard candy, a large ceiling fan
and a black marble soda fountain,
which ran the length of one wall.

As a kid, I passed many summer
afternoons with my friends sitting
at that soda fountain swapping baseball
cards and reading the latest comics.
Doc Raushenbach was a certified pharmacist
though he spent more time mixing
cherry cokes and chocolate shakes
than he did filling prescriptions.
Closing my eyes, I can still see him,
a reticent little man with a German dialect,

steel-rimmed glasses, and a few tufts
of white hair clustered around his ears.
Doc was good to my family.
When my brother drank iodine,
he advised mother to keep
pouring milk down his throat.

The emergency attendants praised
him for his resourcefulness.
Doc was going deaf,
even wore a hearing aid,

but he kept a sharp eye out
for shoplifters—mostly my buddies
pinching candy or bubble gum.
Whenever he'd fill a prescription,
he'd retire to his back room
and they'd swing into action.
But my conscience wouldn't
allow me to join them.
How could I steal from a man
who saved my brother's life?

EPITHALAMION

for Tim and Eileen, August 8, 1992

Marriage is an enchanting rainbow
that suddenly appears, straddling
our lives when we least expect it.
But to enjoy the prismatic colors
we must see it correctly:
With one foot edging the sea
the rainbow reminds us
of the swift tides of time,
life's turbulent water
and the sacrifices love demands.
The arc's other foot,
poised on the mountain top,
provides a vision of the joy
love yields to the faithful.
And if we always remember
to fix our eyes where
the rainbow meets the sky
we will never lose sight
of the beautiful dream
exchanged in our wedding vows.

SPRING MAGIC

Sun-drenched cherry
blossom peeking around
the red brick wall
is harbinger enough
to transform
this grey world
into a pink-white
yellow-green cornucopia
of living color
the ineffable
sleight of hand
of that reliable
old prestidigitator.

PIANO LESSONS

for Betsy and Wes

This was one of those boyhood phases
when passion got the better of me.
So every Saturday morning I'd sit
at the keyboard next to Mrs. Rea
just to be near her *daughter*.
With my attention always divided
I'd rest my stubby fingers
hesitantly on the keys and stare
into those ebony and ivory eyes—
and they would stare back like school nuns
with their habits of black and white
waiting patiently throughout eternity
for the correct spelling.
Tone-deaf ear and untuned fingers
I could never enter Mrs. Rea's world
of Bach, Brahms or Mozart.
Music's language was more mysterious
than a shaman's wisdom
but still I tried the finger-exercises
and counted the scales and minutes
praying to catch a glimpse of her
before the hour was up. I knew
I wasn't destined to be a virtuoso.
Hell, I didn't even own a piano.

III. Under the Wing

Poetry is an orphan of silence.
The words never quite equal the
experience behind them.

—CHARLES SIMIC

SUNSET GEESE

I stand transfixed
feeling like an intruder
that somehow this time
really belongs to them.

A squadron of longnecks
honk their approach
in their customary noisy
celebration of the day's end.

Wings beating furiously
they slip through a seam
in the blood-orange sky
glide in a wide sweeping arc

slowly begin their descent
past a glittering steeple
dark spidery treetops
mute willow branches

before splashing down
in the pond's shadows.

UNDER CROWS

for Sonny

The afternoon hardly breathes
as he jogs the track alone.
Overhead they glide gracefully
moving in their blue theater
like actors in a pantomime.
Dark silent wings circling
like a mobile suspended
by invisible wires
from the immobile sun.
Body moving mind transfixed,
he rides the waves
of light above their wings
to a recurrent dream
of rest security fulfillment
the end of the cycle.
But moving into the shade
under their wings,
he feels life spinning out
like a kite severed
from its string
a speck on the horizon.
Consciousness clouded by doubts
fears irreversible losses,
he remembers his mother's last wish:
to go peacefully in her own bed—
and not among strangers.

LOON

Splashing down in darkness
he shatters the moonlight
on the placid lake.
The night's silence is broken
by his desolate wail.
Like the call of the Banshee
it's an omen recognized
by all suffering humanity:
The gaunt figure in the cancer ward
whose pallid flesh drops off
with each tick of the clock.
The grey mother silently
watching the earth receive
the flag-draped coffin
of her only son.
The rejected figure sitting
in somber shadows staring
at the pulsing neon sign
outside his room waiting
for the release of his soul
from his tormented body.
His fateful dirge concluded
he lifts off the water
wings tilted to the ebony sky
becoming a moon silhouette.

SEA SYMMETRY

White wings silhouetted
against the blue horizon
he knows no boundaries
in his unfettered flight.

Embracing the whitecaps
with undulating motion
he searches for food
in the sea's bounty.

Crying to the wind
with wild exultation
he feels the sunshine dance
with the morning mist.

Seeing his reflected image
in the glistening water
he understands nature's
eternal covenant.

In peaceful equilibrium
between sky and sea,
the seagull lives
in perfect symmetry.

APARTHEID

Walking near the marsh
in the dawn's stillness
he was struck by the sight
of hundreds of crows and gulls
feeding on the wet grass
a checkerboard of black and white
sharing the same space.
Startled by his approach
the birds took flight
a frenzy of feathers
looking for a moment
like a giant winged zebra
gulls flying in one direction
the crows in the other.
Alighting on a bough the crows
cawed wildly down at him.
Settling near the pond's edge
the gulls filled the air
with their infant shrieks.
Amid their violent outcries
the age-old racist heart began
pounding in his breast
like some ancient tribal drum
and he began stoning the crows.

SNOW GEESE

It's a silver January morning.
Walking the snow-covered beach
amid ice-crystals wind-whipped
into tiny tornadoes

exploding upon my face
I watched them honking
across the slate sky
in a perfect V.

Wings tipped upward flapping
furiously in frozen air
they reminded me how rushing blood
can protect against the cold.

As they wing-beat off
to warmer climates casting
their whirling shadow
on the white world below

they seemed to ask why
I wasn't flying with them
leaving this madness called
a New England winter.

NEW ENGLAND

On this frigid
    gray
        day
nothing really matters
    except
        that
steaming bowl
    of
        chowder
on the table
    and
        the
rusty rooster weathervane
    spinning
        wantonly
in
    the
        wind.

WINTER CARDINAL

What're you doing here so soon
you scarlet beauty sitting so smartly
on the snow-covered quince?
You don't have to remind me
those steady horses will soon
be pulling around another season.
At first I thought you
just another Christmas light
until you skittered off
trailing your red streamer.
I must admit, your surprise
visit has flown me right
out of winter.

IV. Crossing the Line

*Nothing factual that I write or
say will be as truthful as my
fiction.*

—NADINE GORDIMER

THE DANCER

At the Friday hop, blue light
reflects off the tinfoil stars
slowly turning back and forth,
a mobile suspended from the ceiling.

While The Platters sing
The Great Pretender, I stand off
in a small circle of guys
practicing a feigned aloofness.

Feet frozen to the gym floor,
I secretly envy the couples dancing.
Blue suede shoes step lightly,
crinoline gowns follow like mirror images.

For a long time I watch them comb
their ducktails, listen to their bravado talk,
but finally, mustering enough courage,
I ask her for a dance.

My stone feet move clumsily
in circles, stiff sweaty hands
keep her at a distance.
Her disapproving eyes tell me

she's discovered my secret:
no rhythm runs in my family blood.
My feet will never learn the art
of keeping time with music.

HER OLD MAN

Writing in their journals
the class was reacting
to Hemingway's story "My Old Man."
In response to a call for volunteers
Sophia said her father was understanding.
Bill's dad taught him sports.
Janet's father was her friend.
Liz said, "I can't write about my old man,
my old man is dead. But I can imagine him.
He wouldn't be ashamed to say
he loved me or show affection in public.
He'd be considerate and bring me flowers.
He would probably apologize for—"
She went mute in mid-sentence.
When she stopped, every eye was on her
and we all died a little in silence.

MONDAY MORNING
WITH MR. ELIOT

Like sand continually eroded
by the expected sea,
Room 612 is filled with a wave
of noisy chattering students.
The scent of chalk dust
mixes with the fetid smell
of someone's leftover lunch
in the wastebasket since Friday.
Facing front, palms leaning
on the desk, the sun glinting
off his glasses, he surveys the room.
"Good morning," they drone lethargically
settling into their seats.
Before his eyes the nightmare begins.
The classroom is slowly transformed
into a mausoleum of bad poetry.
Along the lichen-covered walls
chalk disintegrates like decaying bones
forming neat piles of trite images.

Books crumble to the touch
leaking streams of shredded clichés.
The typewriter sits paralyzed
in grammatical error
atop the metal filing cabinet.
Graffiti slides off desk tops
oozing pools of verbosity

on the cold damp floor.
The twisted hands of the clock
have mangled its face
leaving it as ambiguous
as a mixed metaphor.
Rows of cadaverous students
like silent tombstones
with blank-verse faces
stare at the stuffed pedant.
"Let's turn to 'The Hollow Men'
on page forty-five," he whispers
in a perfunctory manner.

HONKY TONK R&R

Annistan, Alabama, 1957

The band played Country and Western tunes
by Hank and Roy and Elvis, more popular
in the South than church hymns.
I sat at a table near the bandstand,
sipped cold Budweisers, and listened
to the platinum blond sing about
cheatin hearts and born losers.

But I wasn't feeling like a loser
not with several crisp dollar bills
stuffed in my pocket, a weekend pass
and a clean, pressed uniform on my back,
barely visible through the smoke
and haze but conspicuous amid
the cowboy boots, bandannas and jeans.

For a long time I watched them dance,
hips swaying to the guitar's twang,
the tall men in string ties and boots,
hands resting firmly on the rumps
of their big-breasted women
wearing tight skirts and beehives.

The vocalist with the platinum hair,
stacked body shifting from heel
to heel, sings in a hot, husky voice.
I soon become the microphone
within those soft, white fingers,
held so gently to those warm lips.

ON SUNNYSIDE AVENUE

We lived in three rooms
    that we paid for
        under the table

and bought our furniture
    on credit
        one room at a time.

You quit your job
    when the honeymoon
        baby arrived

so I did my juggling act:
    college by day
        bartender by night.

Remember how you use to rock
    yourself to sleep and he'd be awake
        to greet his old man?

Remember how you
    roasted the chicken
        entrails and all

and I locked myself out
    in a blizzard wearing
        only my robe?

Remember how sunlight used to creep
    over the windowsills
        and fill those rooms?

"SUCH STUFF"

for Mary Ellen

When a nurtured dream
breaks off, falls hard
disappears into the earth
like October's leaves,
their motley splendor
only a receding memory,
imagination soon begins
spinning its golden thread
and hope finds life
in the darkness
like night's cold shroud
removed by morning light
restores the roses.

POET

for Joe

In early dawn he slips outside.
He scans the horizon,
imagination taking flight
like a cardinal liberated
from winter's snows.
He puffs on his pipe,

sending images spiraling up
to meet the reddening light
unfolding over the green field.
Several minutes of listening
to the air's silent syllables,
he's pulled inside by the radio's

soulful sound of Bessie Smith.
Back at his desk he releases
the heart's timeless language
onto the computer's blank page,
arranging familiar words
into a brilliant new life.

V. Erin's Magic

*Write well, and there will always
be someone, somewhere who
carries in mind what you have
written.*

—JOHN CIARDI

SPRING REVERIE

for Bridie

White puffs of clouds
like tiny parachutes
drift lazily
across the heavens.
Filtering through a lattice
of branches light forms
a perfect circle of gold
around the old man
whose dreams
like a magnet
are pulled back
to a barefoot boy
in knee breeches
running to school
across a misty pasture
scaring into flight
the morning birds
who envy the piece
of day-old bread clutched
in his tiny hand.

PASSAGES

for John & Bridie

In the early Killarney dawn
we lean on the rail
of a narrow wooden bridge,
listening to the stream's
soft melody, like a flute
heard from a distance.

Underneath the silvery trout
glide in their silent world
as branches of wild fuchsia
drop deep purple blossoms
into the slow-moving water.
One by one the petals

drift toward us, catch
in an eddy and disappear,
like centuries of Irish
forced from the light
of their ancestral land
to travel the world's dark oceans.

CONNOR CROWE'S VIGIL

an Irish folk tale

The moon shines brightly on Kerry's
pebbly beach at Ballyheigh strand
as the surf beats a mournful dirge
against the shadowy recesses of the crag.
Connor sits keeping his eyes peeled
on the coffin resting by the shore.
Occasionally lifting the bottle to combat
the cold and fear, he drifts off
to sleep, watching the moon slip
under the ocean's dark bedspread.
Awakened by a keen, growing louder
and louder by the minute, he's shocked
to see a procession of little undertakers
shouldering the coffin to the family's
burial place: a lost island under Ballyheigh Bay.
Am I sleeping and this merely a dream?
Has the devil whiskey rotted my brain?
Or is this vision the ineffable unity
that sometimes steals upon us when we
least expect it—the sudden glimpse
behind the veil of the invisible world?

A DAUGHTER'S SECRET

for Matthew Quinn

Da's passion was his greyhounds.
Walking to school in the cold dawn,
I'd see him running those dogs
up and down Kerry's misty fields.
He couldn't wait for the Newtown races
to show off Nellie, his favorite.

When Nellie became a celebrity,
winning back-to-back races,
he allowed her into the house
to sit with him by the hearth.
Even now I can see Da's blue eyes
staring into the blazing fire

the proud smile on his face
his strong fingers wrapped around
a whiskey glass, ready to toast
his champion, a contented Nellie
curled at his feet: a green, white, orange
ribbon dangling proudly from her neck.

Da fed his dogs a bran diet
to keep them racing lean and swift.
But my ten-year-old eyes only saw
starvation: bony ribs under tight skin.
Everyday I'd save half my ham or cheese
sandwich and toss it into their kennel.

Da couldn't understand why his dogs
were getting fat and intractable.
When they became distempered,
Mr. Murphy had to put them to sleep.
Before long his dogs were replaced
but my secret's with me forever.

As Mama said, I must've been baptized
with fairy water because I mixed
trouble in my oatmeal every day.

LADY IN BLUE

for Bridie

Grandma died the year I turned seven.
We'd just finished the evening rosary
when Grandma called out Mama's name.
Mama didn't know how much I loved Grandma:
"Girl, you must stop crying. You've kept us up
for three nights. Your Da needs his rest."
That night Da let me sleep in Grandma's bed.
When the Good Lady visited, she was wearing
a blue veil that matched the color of her eyes.
Her voice was soft and gentle: "Dry your tears,
little one, don't cry. Your grandma is with us."
I reached to touch her, but she disappeared.
"Mama, I saw the Good Lady last night."
Then I told Da that Mary's mama called me
a little saint, but Da said it was just silly talk.
Vision or dream? To this day I can't be sure.
But I never cried again for Grandma. I knew
she was with the Good Lady and her Son.

CLUAIN AOIBHIM:
THE BEAUTIFUL MEADOW

for Mary and Maurice

I look out the window
at the crest of Croagh Patrick
where the Saint fasted centuries before.
The sun spins across the eastern sky,
burns off the morning mist
and filters through treetops,
glittering like emeralds.
Sparkling streams slip softly
between gray rocks winding homeward
to the clear water of Clew Bay.
Pressing my ear to the mountain's silence,
I listen for the saintly words
of the heart.

THE SECRET

for Pat

I peer in the window
of the mysterious cottage
hidden in the glen.
Inside the wee folk are festive.

One with a fiddle tucked
under his chin plays furiously.
Another pulls on a squeeze box.
The rest dance jigs and reels
around the musicians.

In the shadows beyond
the hearth's lambent glow
you sit at a loom like Penelope
spinning our love into fine gold.
I'll keep your secret if you promise

never to undo what you've woven.

FLIGHT

for Pat

Invisible hands toss ring clouds
around Killarney's mountain tops
as the twilight sprinkles its
remaining gold upon the earth.
Light shimmers on the mane
of a solitary white stallion
munching tufts of green grass
a few feet from the pasture fence.
With curious eyes, he looks at us.
I call to him and he turns away,
strong flanks shivering slightly.
But her voice entices him over,
the siren song of a flute
carried on a summer breeze.
I try touching his powerful neck,
but he pulls back indifferently.
Then she gently caresses his
forehead and whispers into his ear,
like a Celtic harp strummed softly.
Quivering with joy, he bows
in the presence of his Venus
and receives her gift gratefully.
At any moment, I expect him
to sprout wings and carry her
off across the Irish sky.

FAMILY BURIAL GROUND

near the Cliffs of Moher

We walk the seaside graveyard.
Thunder rumbles, black clouds drift
across the gray western sky
and the Irish Sea angrily spews
white foam against Moher's cliffs.
Lichen spills down the Celtic crosses,
leaning willy-nilly amid the weeds.
As we silently read the surnames—
Cleary, Mulvihill, Quinn—
the dead whisper their soul secrets.
Our hearts speak the ancient sorrow—
a longing for what once was flesh
but now has turned to clay.

VI. Thorns and Roses

Occasional poems are not as powerful as those that come out of a deep need or conviction. Those poems that come out come out because they have to come out.

—RITA DOVE

COMBUSTION

She turns
her face to me
softly covers my hand
flames burning bright behind those eyes.
Oh dear!

TRYST

The beginning is innocent enough
whispers, sighs, embracing eyes
wooden declarations before
more serious sofa explorations.
Groping patting rubbing leading
to a warm tub filled with bath oil
reciting Donne—
but they're not done
until he carries her to fresh white sheets.
Her, with perfumed breasts uptilted
him, with wet silver tongue
they slip and slide in search
of Marvel's pleasures
hoping time will dissolve—
but really anticipating
the emptiness
over coffee and cake.

PLMYERS

for Pat

I open the curtain.

The sun fills the window
becoming her spotlight.
Like the audience waiting

in hushed excitement
before a single word is spoken
I admire my leading lady,

hair nestled on the pillow
sleeping motion of her breast
rising and falling.

My touch becomes the prologue.

On cue she turns to me
anticipating the romantic scene
we've rehearsed so often.

AFTER A TIME

We do not love
one another any more.
Fire consumed us
for a while leaving
only smoldering embers
occasionally fanned
into a soft lambent glow.
But people and years
came between us
like winter ice covers
the lake's beauty
a gradual freezing over
of hearts afire.
Yet images sometimes
make me remember
like burning wood
after a snowfall
and ice crystals
clinging to roses
after the first frost.

THAT MOMENT

for Pat

As night gradually gives way
to gray and the sun steps
from behind the rose blush curtain,
flames across the eastern sky,
envelops me in its sacred light,
so your light protects me
from the approaching darkness
as we drift quietly closer
to that moment
when time holds still.

PROMISES

Sometimes when I lie down to sleep
snippets of old conversations
come back to me like a thief
entering quietly in the dark.
Oh how we talked
after the martinis and candlelight
walking under that rhinestone canopy,
which we mistook for diamonds,
with the moon like a god
pressing his ear against the starry wall
overhearing the whispered vows
of sanctified conspirators.
But the promises made
as we lay down to love
letting our carousel hearts
race faster and faster
reaching for brass-ring dreams
far into the night.
Only the sunlight glistening
on the brass bedpost
made all those promises
seem like empty words.

SUMMER MORNING

The night has been unbearable
like scorching sand
like scalding water.
Waking on a bed of nails
head throbbing splitting
like an axe embedded in a log
I feel the brooding stillness
the charred grass indifferently
turning to brown ashes
the withered rose exposing
its thorns to the sizzling light
the cacophony of insects
crazy with heat
my lover gone.

SUNBURST

for Pat

In the afterglow of day,
when the Irish sun gets pressed
between dark rain clouds and Killarney's
green mountain tops—and erupts,
raining flecks of fire upon the lake,
when the blue surface flickers and ignites,
setting in motion nymphs wearing
silver tights who spin cartwheels
across the flashing water,
when they remove their golden bracelets
and toss them to the silent shore,
turning a meadow of wildflowers
into an epiphany of light,
I think of you.

DISSOLUTIONS

for Pat

The way evening
comes so quickly
quietly filling the spaces
between still branches
until the tree's assimilated
into the astral night
so I watch you
slowly, gently cover
my dark spaces, enveloping
me in your calm
until we're ready
to take our places
among the drifts of stars.

LOVE'S CYCLE

When summer has
turned to winter
noon to night
when harmony gives
way to dissonance
order to confusion
I will know
your hands have
turned white
and cold
and I will
bleed silently
alone.

VII. Midpoint

*The way poetry has of setting our
internal houses in order, of
formalizing emotion difficult to
articulate, is one of the reasons
we still depend on it in moments
of crisis.*

—MARK STRAND

APRIL MOON

This evening the moon,
so full and yellow,
lies balanced on top
or our old elm,
a large delicious apple.
I'm going to take a paring knife
climb onto the roof and peel
off the brilliant skin.
When the last scrap of parings
falls away, I'll slice the flesh
into halves, quarters, then sections,
and scatter the golden pieces
across the early spring sky.

NIGHT PEOPLE

Midnight at the supermarket
a weary old black woman, torn stockings
rolled up to her knees, waddles a shopping cart
down the deserted aisle.

Park light dim thru twisted branches
the widower walks his dog
feeling the night chill
alone with his shadow and memories.

Beneath the illicit stars they stroll
indifferent streets of strange towns
knowing the jagged night of reality
will shatter their secret illusion.

Moonlight reflecting on the rooftop
he looks at the tiny serpent lights
crawling below seconds away
from floating forever in darkness.

He sits in the dark room praying
to the blinking neon sign
for the release of his soul
from his tormented body.

In the smoke-grey dawn the old sailor
spread-eagled on the city concrete
dreams of naked women pointing the bow
to open seas and exotic lands.

PINE SIGHT:
THIRTEEN REFRACTIONS

after Wallace Stevens

The young pine bends
and sways cooling itself
in the spring shower.

A doe enters the pine thicket
making tracks on the spongy
cushion of wet needles.

In the late afternoon
a mockingbird warbles unseen
in the pine's green arms.

A warm summer breeze diffuses
honeysuckle and sweetgrass
through the pine copse.

A slash pine stands in the dark
listening to a concerto
of cicadas, katydids and toads.

Pine trees cool the humid air.
A squirrel pauses
under the dark canopy.

Pushing aside the darkness
the sun splinters light
through pine branches.

The chandelier is reflected
on the chapel window.
Beyond a pine wears a golden crown.

Lightning flashes
and the pinetop explodes
in a burst of flame.

Weary with winter
a pine drops white globules
from its heavy limbs.

A solitary pine stands
on the ridge wearing
its soft white robe.

Leaning over the frozen lake
a pine falls in love
with its own image.

Bark crackles and drips
in the fiery hearth.
A pine log burns to ash.

COMIC RELIEF

When you come shambling in
with bright cherry nose
soulful eyes and painted frown,
alone in the center
of the circular light
dragging that absurd broom,
we laugh at your hopelessness.
String-pulling in one ear
out the other, you're
the obligatory clown relieving
our fears and anxieties—
the daily high wire act.
We think it's hilarious
you sweeping the spotlight
smaller and smaller until
you finally disappear.
After all, it's not our
loneliness and extinction
we're watching.

NOCTURNAL MUSIC

Sultry summer heat
sticks to my skin
night sounds crickets
barking dogs sirens
foghorn trapped
in my skull
images flickering
on and off the screen
afraid to pull
down the shade
of consciousness
might never hear
another bird.

SATURDAY NIGHT

After dinner, it's dancing
with four old friends
who've recently lost spouses.
Lifted by notes pouring
from an alto sax we gyrate
around the floor in defiance
of our aging bodies.
Forehead sweat beads, then runs,
as we swing free of time
and gravity for a few hours.
Weaving through smoke
and warm bodies, we sit one out.
Then smiles and laughter
and golden beers before
we begin to sense the fears
of four desperate people:
One fears retirement,
the other an early death.
The women fear the lonely
lives of widow and divorcee.
And we, like always, fear
the unexpected wrenching
of our giddy happiness,
tossing us into an ocean
of breakers rising in darkness.

SOBRIETY

Jesus, how difficult
    it is
        to pass up
those moments
    when you get out
        of that stranger's body
and begin to like
    the sound
        of your own voice
and talk to yourself
    in the language
        of moonlight and dreams
and listen hard
    to the old stories
        the old lies
and laugh
    like a carefree
        young child
before you wake
    inside the old flesh
        and cry.

SHELTER COVE

for Jan & Bruce

Neptune's statue stands watch
over furled masts pushing upward
through a pink-blue twilight.
Marina boat bells disturb the serenity.
Couples promenading along the harbor
watch a Carolina sun reeled across
glittering water—a golden carp.
As stars wake from their slumber
a modern-day troubadour sings
songs of love—a night
of symmetry and transcendence.

MORTAL THOUGHTS

Some might call us the lucky ones
happily, carelessly dancing through life.
But recently we're more serious about death
though we haven't formally invited him in
or even hinted where we keep the spare key.
Nowadays we don't dare travel
without thinking of a will or talking
to him daily through the obituary column—
yet always in an offhand manner.
What he's told us is not very pleasant:
How our lives will remain unwritten
a mystery without form and clues.
How we will continue to cram our days
with poetry, music, natural pleasures
to forget the hour when he will come
uninvited and unannounced.

VIII. Portraits

Poetry is the antidote to technology.

—OCTAVIO PAZ

VINCENT AT ARLES

Down by a river
he calmly sits painting
the undulating wheatfield brilliant
under a tranquil Provençal sun.

Without warning thunder clouds
move in and a storm begins.
In the field the peasants,
who were observing him,
run for shelter. Lightning flashes,
strikes a cypress nearby,
and the tree explodes in flames.

But he remains painting.
His brushstrokes move feverishly
keeping pace with the wind's violence.
A curtain of rain hisses on the water
and the wheatfield becomes a raging sea,
seething and whorling in his hand.

Later, in the tavern, eyes shining
water dripping from his beard
grotesque ear illuminated
by the hearth's light, he sits alone
feeling the warmth of the cognac.

Across the room peasants whisper
as they circulate a petition,
confining him to a barred cell
in the Arles hospital.

OLD J. ALFRED

The old man leans out the window
in shirt sleeves and listens
to the vernacular of a gull
disturb the afternoon stillness.
He observes spring blossoming
under those white wings
that perform a sky ballet
before gliding to rest atop a piling.
A lighthouse pushes through clouds
sending sunbursts glittering
on the jeweled sea as children wade
in the surf skipping stones
across the water and wait
for the couple who stroll the beach.
But for him loneliness hangs
in the air like the crucifix
hanging on his bedroom wall.
When the white wings flap off
the reverie ends leaving him
to his world of books, faded photographs
half-forgotten dreams of silent seas.

ELPENOR'S POSTWAR
STRESS DISORDER

The youngest was Elpenor...[who], having climbed
on Circe's roof to taste the cool of night, fell
asleep with wine. Waked by our morning
voices, and the tramp of men below, he
started up, but missed his footing on
the long steep backward ladder and
fell that height headlong.

—THE ODYSSEY

We'll be pushing our prow
toward Ithaca at dawn.
Under the flickering light
of Circe's hall they sit, old warriors
savoring their wine, swapping
war stories, thinking of home.
I sit alone already sinking
in an alcoholic sea.

A naive farm boy dreaming
of glory when I enlisted,
the army has been my family—
Odysseus my only father.
They don't know it but more
of their fathers are dying each day
and they will soon follow.
The war has left me nothing

except the darkness gathering
around me, pressing me on all sides,
keeping the light from my soul.
Then the images appear:
Riderless horses, manes on fire,
rush madly through flames,
hooves kicking up dust and death.
Carrion birds fly with bloody beaks.

Fiery arrows hiss into flesh,
scorching it black as crows.
Chariots clatter over bits of bones,
bleached white in the sunlight.
A volley of spears silently soar,
some clang off shields,
others pierce human hearts,
which flutter like dying fish.

Flush with the wine's heat, I climb
to Circe's roof. My soul rises
from under the dark sea,
mingles with the moonlight,
bursts into flame, sending flakes
of light swirling with the stars.
He kept his promise
and gave me a soldier's burial.

KENNEBUNKPORT ARTIST

She sits at the bar
of the cozy pub fingering
a brandy incongruous
among the workmen drinking
their mid-day beer.

Beret cocked rakishly
aside short-cropped hair
scarf hiding a petite neck
she stares at her image
in the large mirror.

The workmen chattering
about broken sewer lines
and the Red Sox are impervious
to her detailed seascapes
adorning the walls.

Does she see wasted youth
too many hours spent
at the easel and palette?

Has she been deceived
by fame or fortune
evanescent as the smoke
curling to the ceiling?

Perhaps she's happy
being the silent curator
of this makeshift gallery?

EX-CHAMP

for Muhammad Ali

Must have been the whispers
that drew his attention.
Slowly lifting his face
he returns the crowd's gaze.

Looking into those eyes
We wonder which image
gives comfort to his soul:

His arm raised in triumph
he bends his youthful neck
to get the gold medal

Thrilling the cheering crowd
he dances and stings foes
under the bright light's glare

In the mosque's late shadows
a proud man kneels alone
and studies the Koran?

His eyes once so alive
and sparkling seem now just
reminders of the dark
history of his race.

THE WIDOW
ON SHERWOOD ROAD

I told the kids I'd be just fine
in my own house, with my bed, phone
with my color TV and blue bedspread
so much to do to keep busy.

Now, I sit in the dark and wait
for dawn to break working the beads
saying Hail Marys for each one
from Kerry to Connecticut.

After, I sit in the kitchen
with my coffee waiting for the
same old mail listening to the
tick tock and voices of children.

Later, I sit in the old den
in front of my TV watching
the game shows and waiting for the
phone to ring, so I can say, "Yes."

I don't forget, not for a moment
but I keep busy—and time moves.

IRISH PATRIOT

for John

The coffin is draped
with the orange white green banner
a gift from the I.R.A.
It's a typical Irish wake
but the man wasn't.
He was an original
fighting the Black and Tans
in Erin's struggle for independence.
On his chest Little Jack,
as his compatriots called him,
wears the Campaign Medal
a symbol of the battles
imprisonment, hunger strikes
he left behind.
But those who knew him
in his adopted country
remember a soldier for peace
a man of faith who touched all
with love and good will.
Above, the sunlight spears
a rosary of grey clouds.
Below, Little Jack is lowered
to his final rest
as a solitary piper wails
the Soldier's Song.

MEMORIAL DAY

for J.C., two Vietnam tours,
Bronze Star, three Purple Hearts

Beneath the naked bulb
of the lonely room
tragic with the look
of drugs and tears
he lay spread-eagled
across the American flag.
Could he be the same marine
who shipped home from Nam?
Wasn't he an imposing figure
standing tall in sergeant stripes
marching into the future confidently
with a chest full of ribbons?
But that was yesteryear.
Today his scorched soul found release
from his tormented body.

He already had burned the ribbons.

WEST POINT CEMETERY

> *Were you to fail, a million ghosts in olive drab,*
> *in brown khaki, in blue and gray would rise*
> *from their white crosses, thundering those*
> *magic words: duty, honor, country.*
> —GENERAL DOUGLAS MACARTHUR

An old man pulls up in a black
limousine, to perform his last duty.
The gray warrior walks among
a battalion of silent comrades,
their white crosses arrayed
across the frozen ground.
Epaulets of snowflakes collect
on his shoulders. He pauses to read
the tablets, weathered to a blank slate,
some as old as the country itself.
Lifting his hand for a final salute,
he knows his fame won't be erased
as quickly as the fading words
on these snow-covered slabs.

IX. Conclusions

*I have tried to write the best I
can; sometimes I have good luck
and write better than I can.*

—ERNEST HEMINGWAY

"NOTHING GOLD CAN STAY"

He thought he had misunderstood
the hospital receptionist
when she told him the wing.

In the white aseptic maternity ward
a father was tapping
on the nursery window.
Hysterectomy patients were just beyond.

In the vase roses
he had sent were wilting
in the sterile room.

She was lying awake
in the unsettled darkness.
He kissed her gently
but words were stones.

So they began
the last chapter silently—
like grass when the wind stops.

WINTER OBLATION

for Jim Leary, May 14, 1994

Smoke rising from chimneys
like altar incense meets
the falling snow and fills
the air with the heavenly
scent of burning wood.

Myriads of swirling flurries
encircle a solitary steeple
its gold cross offered up
to a slate-grey sky.

On the hillside still
shapes of twisted elms
wear their white mantle
like snow-covered crosses
in a New England cemetery.

One courageous seagull
spread wings barely visible
amid the blinding brilliance
hangs motionless watching

the glistening crystals
floating downward exploding
their purity on dark rooftops
telephone wires blacktopped streets
turning the earth

into a reflection
of the honest soul.

NIGHT RIDE

Awake at two A.M.
I sit in the darkness
numbed by the loss
of our two close friends.
The stubborn moon
is framed in our window
and the refracted light
through the blinds
resembles a silver escalator
leading to our back door.
Jesus, how I want to step
on that escalator and cry
all the way to the top floor.

UNDERSTANDING

His room is intact
exactly like he left it
the night he died.
Shoes neatly arranged
under the bed
books trophies posters
never collecting dust
fresh flowers always
on the nightstand.
Sometimes she even sets
an extra plate or talks
to the smiling photograph.
Truth is, I could never understand
why she's kept his ghost
locked up in that room
for so many years—
that is, until today
when I found the withered rose
taken from my father's coffin
pressed between the pages
of the family album.

HIGH SCHOOL REUNION

Like noisy excited fans
at the finish line
we gathered
for the outcome.
Many favorites failed
to get out of
the starting blocks.
Over half had false starts
ending in divorce court.
A couple of longshots
were surprisingly
outrunning the field
burning their cinders
down the stretch.
Several pulled up lame
needing support
in their final drive
into the tape.
A few had already
dropped out.

NEW YEAR'S PARTY

Amid the proper faces
warm feelings running tongues
imaginations are alive
with unfulfilled fantasies.
They greet and mingle toasting
good health and an end
to meetings greed profits.
As time slowly dissolves
Auld Lang Syne floats
to the ceiling enveloping
the players like a tinsel dome.
He sits at the table and shares
their bread and wine storing
images celebrating life
forgiving their humanity.

LAST LESSON

for J.B., October 31, 1993

Why the welcome home balloons
walls of get well wishes
and make-shift wooden ramp
for this fancy new wheelchair

while I fight back tears
of self-pity
like those feigning an optimism
they don't really feel?

Why can't I recognize
the stick figure wearing
my clothes or the voice speaking
from me like old radio static

during long sleepless nights
as I search for meaning
in the unequivocal eyes
of that stuffed bear beside the bed?

Why do I already know
what those eyes are trying to say?
In dying pride dissolves—but love
conquers a despairing heart

releasing the honest soul.

WINTER WALK

I crunch along the moonlit roads.
Under the streetlight snowflakes
swarming like bees
brush gently against my face.

I hear happy voices
of children playing tag
shovels scraping across concrete
the barking of a curious dog
bells chiming hymns
from the First Congregational.

A snowplow approaches
piling snow on either side
like a dangerous behemoth
with pulsing red eyes.

With moonlight illuminating
the stained glass window
of St. Paul's Episcopal Church
the crucifixion scene looms
large and compelling.

Like woodsmoke rising
in the winter night
my soul floats among the stars.

LETTING GO

When those old vacuous eyes
dimmed blinked once—shut
only memories remained.
He wanted to go with her
be faithful to the end.
He had to know the meaning
of her resignation submission
willingness to travel
this silent journey.
But the gold wedding band
slipping off her finger
told him everything
he needed to know.

CONFESSION

He's totally incompetent
about almost everything.
Never ask him
to repair the car
or stop a leaky faucet.
A hammer's a dangerous
weapon in his hand
and anything electrical
remains as mysterious
as the alchemist's wisdom.
Yet—there are times
he's fixed the earth
with only a word or touch.